Dressage

HOW TO...

HowToDressage.com

**The Pocket Book of Dressage Exercises**

ISBN: 9798707676178

Requests to publish work from this book should be sent to:
**hello@howtodressage.com**

THE
# POCKET
BOOK OF
# DRESSAGE
# EXERCISES

# CONTENTS

# INTRODUCTION

When riding in a bare dressage area, it can be very easy to get stuck trotting around the outside track, repeating the same exercises and patterns over and over again.

To help you spice things up a bit, we have put together 30 dressage exercises complete with diagrams and examples of how you can vary the exercises to meet your horse's level of training.

...and since this book is pocket-sized, you can take it with you wherever you go!

Now, although it can be tempting to just crack-on and get going, to help you get the most out of this book, make sure you read the following sections before you start:

- Notes before you begin    page 2
- Your job as the rider – page 4
- The scales of training – page 8

If you get stuck with any of the terminology or movements, you'll find a handy glossary at the back of this book. You can also visit our website HowToDressage.com should you want a more detailed breakdown of how to ride a specific movement.

We hope you find this compact book a useful training tool in your daily dressage training.

*How To Dressage x*

# NOTES BEFORE YOU BEGIN

- All the diagrams in the book are based on a short 20mx40m arena. However, you can adapt the exercises to fit a long 20mx60m arena if you want to.

- Note that all diagrams are not drawn to an exact scale, although they are as accurate as we can make them.

- Although it's not essential, we recommend that you buy (or make) some arena letters and lay them out as accurately as you can. (Arena measurements can be found on page 20) Riding to the letters teaches you to be accurate, which is crucial to gain maximum marks in a dressage test. Also, accurately riding the exercises in this book means you'll get the full benefit from them.

- We've devised all the exercises and floorplans in this book so that they can be ridden in walk, trot, and canter. Please feel free to modify or combine any of the exercises to suit your horse's ability and current level of training. We have given you some examples of how to do this in the 'Variations' section, but feel free to create your own.

- Before you begin working on any of the exercises in this book, make sure that you warm-up your horse and yourself properly to avoid injuries.

- Throughout your schooling sessions, always keep the dressage Scales of Training in the forefront of your mind (see page 8).

- If things don't go to plan and your horse struggles with an exercise, take a step back and ask him something easier that he's comfortable with before moving on to more challenging work.

- When working on any of the exercises and floorplans in the book, ride them on both reins equally. Most horses are more supple on one side than the other, so don't be tempted to ride more on the "easy" side, or your horse won't develop evenly on both reins.

- If your horse lacks suppleness and balance, or is at the beginning of their training, be prepared to make the circles larger if necessary.

- Keep your schooling sessions fresh and interesting for you and your horse; don't drill the same exercise continually. Instead, mix and match the exercises and try connecting some together to create a longer, more challenging routine.

- If your horse loses his balance or makes a mistake, take a moment to re-group and correct him before continuing. Don't feel the need to carry on regardless; you are not riding a test.

- Dressage can be very intense, and your horse will tire quickly, especially if he's young or new to the discipline. So, be sure to allow plenty of walk and stretching breaks.

- When you have finished working your horse, remember to allow him to cool down and stretch so that he doesn't stiffen up and become sore later.

# YOUR JOB AS THE RIDER

It's important to remember that your horse is only half of the partnership, and in order for him to do his job to the best of his ability, you need to hold up your end of the team.

Here are some things that you need to keep in mind:

1.  Choose exercises suitable for your horse's training level so that you don't overface your horse and damage his confidence.

2.  If things go wrong, don't struggle on. Go back to something that your horse finds comfortable and take small steps toward the more challenging work.

3.  Have a clear plan of what you want to achieve from your schooling sessions, e.g., more suppleness to the bend, sharper transitions, better uphill balance, etc. Choose exercises and floorplans designed to improve those areas to get the most benefit from the work.

4.  Focus on small details. So, ride accurately, have the correct bend, make the horse straight, etc.

5.  Be patient when teaching your horse new exercises and school figures to keep the learning fun and prevent your horse from becoming tense and resentful.

6.  Have the dressage Scales of Training uppermost in your mind when schooling your horse, i.e., Rhythm, Suppleness, Contact, Impulsion, Straightness, Collection. (Page 8)

7. Look up and not down at your horse's neck. Your head is the heaviest part of your body. If you look down, the weight of your head will cause your shoulders to slump, tipping your weight onto your fork and pushing your horse onto his forehand.

8. Look ahead to the next marker so that you get into the habit of always riding the exercises accurately.

9. Ensure that you are always sitting in the center of your saddle, over your horse's center of gravity.

10. Maintain the ear-shoulder-hip-heel alignment, keeping your shoulders relaxed and down and your pelvis upright. That means you're using the minimum amount of effort to remain in balance.

11. Ensure that you're sitting on the flat area of your pelvis, i.e., the part that's between your seat bones and pubic bone. That prevents you from tipping backward into a "chair seat" or forward into a "fork seat," both of which make you unstable and ineffective.

12. Make sure that your stirrups are the correct length so that you don't lose your balance. For dressage riding, you need to have a bend at the knee. Take your feet out of your stirrups. Ideally, the stirrup tread should hang alongside your ankle. However, if your leg feels unsecure in this position, shorten your stirrups a few holes. The most important aspect is that your leg is effective.

13. Keep your shoulders and hips in line with those of your horse so that you don't twist, which would make your body crooked, upsetting the horse's balance and straightness.

14. Follow the horse's movement in all paces so that you don't disrupt the rhythm or block the impulsion through the horse's back.

15. In rising trot, make sure that you are riding on the correct diagonal so that you don't unbalance the horse.

16. Use half-halts to prepare and balance the horse for each change of pace and direction.

17. Keep a straight line from your elbow, through your wrists, down your reins to your horse's mouth. Ensure that your shoulders and elbows remain relaxed and soft so that you offer the horse a constant, elastic contact to work into.

18. Keep both your wrists upright and don't turn them over or flatten them. That causes "piano hands" and presents the horse with a fixed, blocking contact.

19. Carry your hands as a pair, slightly above, in front of, and at the same width as the horse's withers.

20. Check that your reins are the correct length so that you can maintain a consistent contact with your horse's mouth. If your reins are too long, your communication with the horse will be fragmented, and he will be unable to work into a correct, elastic connection. If your reins are too short, you will create tension and a fixed, blocking contact.

21. Ride forward to keep the horse's hind leg activated and underneath him.

22. Ride accurately to get the maximum benefit from the exercises and to prepare yourself for riding a dressage test.

23. Know when it's time to end the schooling session and always end on a positive note. That way, you and your horse both have fun and don't become stale or soured by schooling.

# THE SCALES OF TRAINING

The six Scales of Training are what the riders in one of the world's most successful dressage nations are taught throughout their early years of riding.

The Scales are designed, through systematic training, to create an equine athlete who works in a perfect balance and makes the most of the movement they naturally possess.

The Scales of Training are:

The Training Scales are meant to be approached in this order, although there are occasions when one can be skipped over in order to work on improving another, there are no shortcuts!

For your horse to achieve his maximum potential, it's crucial that you work methodically through the Scales, making steady progress.

## How the scales link to one another

Until your horse is working in <u>Rhythm</u>, he will not be able to become <u>Supple.</u>

Until he is <u>Supple</u>, the <u>Contact</u> will be inconsistent.

Until the <u>Contact</u> is established, <u>Impulsion</u> will not be true.

If the horse is not working through a <u>Supple</u> back, forwards with <u>Impulsion</u> to a consistent, elastic <u>Contact</u>, he will not be <u>Straight.</u>

In the early stages of the horse's training, <u>Collection</u> refers to balance. Only when a horse is established in the preceding five Scales will he be able to become sufficiently <u>Collected</u> (through the half-halt) to perform the advanced work that is demanded by the highest-level tests.

## Your horse's physical wellbeing

Training your horse along the Scales will ensure that he gradually becomes physically supple and strong enough to be able to do the work required at each level without sustaining injury.

A horse that does not learn to carry his rider in a physically functional manner is damaging his body, particularly his leg joints and his spine.

Trying to take shortcuts can cause serious problems for your horse.

For example, pulling the horse's head down into an "outline" will cause him to tighten and hollow his back, trail his hocks, and lose regularity in the rhythm. The horse will usually open his mouth against the contact, tilt his head, or drop behind the vertical to escape the rider's nagging hands. The end result of this scenario is a low mark for the test and a miserable horse with a sore mouth and back!

So, you can see from this example that a correctly trained horse is less likely to sustain long-term physical problems and will be much happier in his work. His dressage career is also likely to be longer than that of the horse whose rider has tried to take shortcuts and damaged their poor horse as a result!

Let's take a look at each of the training scales individually.

---

# 1. RHYTHM

---

As the first of the training scales, we need to have a really clear understanding of what is required before you can consider that you have fulfilled this scale, because without that, moving on to the subsequent scales is pointless.

In short, if your horse does not have rhythm, you have nothing to build upon and no way to progress.

There are three main aspects to rhythm:

1.   Regularity of the beats
2.   Regularity of the correct sequence of footfalls
3.   Tempo – the speed of the rhythm.

As the FEI defines it:
*"The rhythm is the regularity of the beats in all paces. The regularity is the correct sequence of the footfalls and the tempo is the speed of the rhythm."*

Let's take a look at the required rhythm in each of the three paces.

## Walk

A correct walk has four evenly spaced footfalls. If you listen to a horse walking along a road, you should hear 1 – 2 – 3 – 4 beats. A bigger walk will have a slower tempo, although the easiest image of a correct tempo is encapsulated by the old hunting term, 'he looks like he's going home for lunch'. Another way to image it is to picture soldiers marching; purposeful and brisk, but unhurried.

## Trot

The trot pace has a two-beat rhythm.

In the correct sequence at trot, the legs move in coordinated diagonal pairs with a clear moment of suspension between the two sets of footfalls.

As a horse progresses in training, the moment of suspension will increase and become more clearly defined as a result of the horse's improved strength and balance producing more upward thrust, as well as forward travel. This is where the tempo becomes important, as that greater cadence should never become 'dwelling' or 'hovering', but still maintaining its forward impetus.

## Canter

The canter has a three-beat rhythm and the correct sequence of legs is as follows:

- outside hind
- diagonal pair (inside hind and outside fore together)
- inside fore
- followed by a clear moment of suspension (all four feet off the ground)

- The sequence then re-commences.

In right lead canter the right foreleg is the last footfall of the sequence, and vice versa for the left.

As in the trot, the quality of the gait is enhanced by a pronounced moment of suspension, or 'jump', when all four hooves are off the ground, giving the potential for the development of flying changes.

The tempo should be crisp but unhurried.

---

# 2. SUPPLENESS

---

Suppleness is a very broad topic, and there are many aspects of your horse's training to which the term can be applied.

The importance of suppleness is reflected in its place in the scales of training – second, only after rhythm. But when you consider that we are talking about whole body suppleness (and we should even include mental suppleness in there as well) you might begin to get an inkling of the size of the topic.

To split suppleness down into smaller chunks, consider:

- Longitudinal suppleness – top line, to include back, neck, poll, and jaw.
- Lateral suppleness – even and equal bend to the two sides
- Suppleness of the joints – essential for activity and ability to engage (weight carry)

- Mental suppleness – full acceptance of the aids, without any resistance

The areas are all interlinked, and you will find that as one improves, others will do too.

Suppleness must be a central theme throughout schooling and should be constantly checked and reinforced at all stages.

To be truly supple, your horse must be relaxed both physically and mentally, and the image you are seeking is of the horse moving through its whole body, not just with its legs – what we call *'a body mover'* as opposed to *'a leg mover'*.

---

# 3. CONTACT

---

The FEI definition of contact states:
*"Contact is the soft, steady connection between the rider's hand and the horse's mouth. The horse should go rhythmically forward from the rider's driving aids and 'seek' contact with the rider's hand, thus 'going into' the contact."*

It is, therefore, important to understand that it's the horse that *seeks* the rider's hand, and the rider who, in turn, grants it.

Attempting to impose a contact in order to place the horse's head 'in an outline' will only cause the horse to break his neck at the third or fourth vertebra. This then becomes the highest point, rather than the poll.

The outline and the contact with the rider's hand come from the impulsion and the horse's willingness to work forward and over his back.

Your contact should never exceed the amount of energy being generated by the horse's hind legs. Your hand should receive only what your leg puts into it.

Good practice for the rider is to consider that the rein contact originates in the horse's mouth and terminates in the rider's elbows with the hand as a modifier en route. With this concept, pulling on the reins becomes a thing of the past, as the elbows should never move behind the rider's body, and as a result, the energy in the system is never blocked by the rein contact.

Your hands, wrists, elbows, and shoulders should all 'breathe' with the horse's movement, rather than remaining fixed and rigid.

Developing a good elastic contact takes time and patience, but it will be worth the effort in the end.

---

# 4. IMPULSION

---

The FEI defines impulsion as:
*"The transmission of controlled, propulsive energy generated from the hindquarters into the athletic movement of the eager horse. Its ultimate expression can be shown only through the horse's soft and swinging back, and is guided by the gentle contact with the rider's hand."*

You can see within that definition how the scales of suppleness (scale no. 2) and contact (scale no. 3) are essential for the control and direction of impulsion into a useful tool.

Asking for too much impulsion before scales one to three are established can cause problems, as the horse will not yet have the physical ability to manage a lot of impulsion without stiffening or coming against the hand. He should be forward-thinking and reactive to your driving aids but beware of pushing him for an inappropriate amount of impulsion too early on.

The results of the right amount of impulsion at the right time in the horse's training results in:
- an increased amount of power and ability to produce a range of variations within the paces,
- an increased amount of thrust and ability to spring off the ground in trot and canter,
- an increased amount of suspension and cadence,
- and an impression of controlled power.

---

## 5. STRAIGHTNESS

---

Try to think of straightness in the following terms to gain a better understanding.

1. 'Straightness' is rather a misnomer, a better word to use is 'alignment'.
2. The forefeet must be aligned with the hind feet on straight and curved lines.
3. The horse should have equal bend (and hence, alignment) on both reins.

Although straightness may not be a priority in the earlier stages, you need to start paying attention to it from the word go.

Straightening natural crookedness takes months and years of persistent work, and although you may not *achieve* it until the horse is relatively advanced in training terms, you will need to work on it as an underlying issue pretty much as soon as your basic controls are established.

The FEI defines straightness like this:
*"The horse is straight when its forehand is in line with its hindquarters, that is, when the longitudinal axis is in line with the straight or curved track it is following"*.

To simplify a little, just picture your horse's spine, and line that up to the line you are following.

If would like to take things a bit further, you have two types of straightness:

1. absolute straightness
2. functional straightness

*Absolute* straightness is what you are trying to achieve on a center line. You want your horse's spine to be totally aligned to the straight line along which you are riding, from his head, along his neck, along his back, and into his hindquarters and tail with no part of his body deviating off the line.

*Functional* straightness needs a little more explanation. Your horse's hips are wider than his shoulders. This means that if you are riding on soft ground and you look at the imprint of his front and hind hooves, you will see that the front feet land on the ground slightly closer together than the hind feet, so although we talk about alignment as the front and hind hooves traveling in the same lines, this is not quite possible.

Functional straightness describes when you have the two hooves (front and back of one side) traveling along the same line and is what you should strive to achieve in canter.

---

# 6. COLLECTION

---

Collection is the re-balancing of the horse carrying the foreign weight of the rider teaching him to carry more of the (combined) weight on his hind quarters than on his shoulders. This makes him more balanced and able to perform ridden movements with ease and in a beautiful and biomechanically functional carriage that gives the appearance of traveling uphill.

Quoting the FEI (and British Dressage), the aim of collection is:
*"To further develop and improve the equilibrium of the horse, which has been more or less displaced by the additional weight of the rider. To develop and increase the horse's ability to lower and engage its hindquarters for the benefit of the lightness and mobility of its forehand. To add to the 'ease and carriage' of the horse, thereby making it more pleasurable to ride."*

Collection refers to differences in:
- Stride length (shorter)
- Stride height (taller)
- Overall balance – with more weight clearly distributed to the hindquarters rather than the shoulders

- A shorter, taller outline as a result of the above change in weight distribution (i.e., *not* because you've just shortened the reins and pulled the neck higher).

As you can see, collection is not about cramming your horse together between stronger rein and leg aids to create smaller steps; it is the gradual development of the ability and strength to carry more weight behind and less on the shoulders, with the above differences as a *consequence* of collection, and not the other way around.

The degree of collection required in dressage tests at each level must be sufficient to enable the horse to perform the required movements with ease and fluency. So, at the lower levels when collection is first introduced, that's not much. All the judge is looking for is that the horse can bring his weight enough off his shoulders to be able to, for example, perform a 10-meter circle without struggling, or make a downward transition from canter to walk without pitching forward and putting all his weight onto either his front feet or the reins.

The higher the level, the higher the degree of collection required, until at the top levels you have enough to produce, for example, a canter pirouette in balance and with visible ease.

Collection is the culmination of all of your training.

---

**For more detailed information on the Scales of Training, along with how to improve upon each building block, please visit our website HowToDressage.com**

## Free Email Training Courses

- **Dressage Newbie Email Course** – A course designed for those who are new to dressage.
  https://howtodressage.com/newbiecourse

- **Dressage Competition Email Course** – A course for riders who are new to competitive dressage.
  https://howtodressage.com/competitioncourse

- **Scales of Training Email Course** – A course looking at each of the training scales in depth.
  https://howtodressage.com/scalescourse

## Free Download

- **7 Simples Steps to Boost Your Dressage Scores** –
  https://howtodressage.com/7steps

# 20X40 SHORT ARENA DIMENSIONS

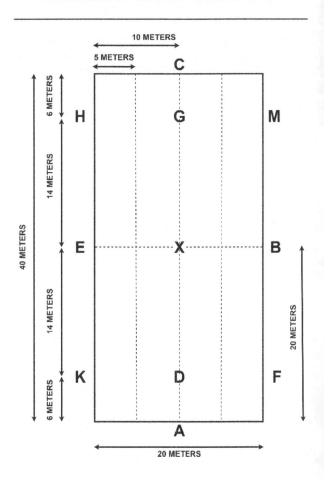

# 20X60 LONG ARENA DIMENSIONS

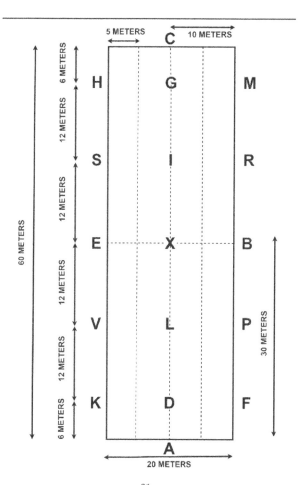

# EXERCISE 1

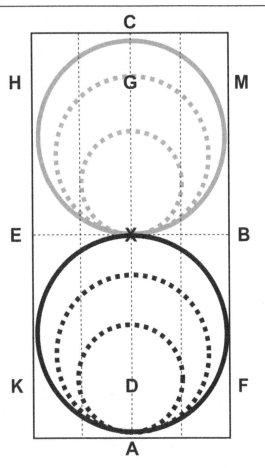

**THE BRIEF:**

Ride three circles at A. First, ride a 20-meter circle, then a 15-meter circle, and finally a 10-meter circle.

These should be three, clearly-ridden separate circles; not a large circle that drifts into a smaller one.

---

**VARIATIONS:**

- 20-meter circle in canter. 15-meter circle in trot. 10-meter circle in walk. Each time transitioning at A.
- 20-meter circle in a medium pace e.g., medium trot. 15-meter circle in a working pace e.g., working trot. 10-meter circle in a collected pace e.g., collected trot.
- Ride the circle at X to add difficulty and to test accuracy.

---

**NOTES:**

- The size and shape of the circle must be accurate and ridden at the prescribed marker. Notice the difference between a circle and riding into the corners.
- The horse must travel on one track and show a clear, correct, uniform bend through his body.
- The rhythm must be correct and in a suitable tempo (speed).
- Maintain the impulsion and uphill balance, especially on the smaller circles.
- If riding in canter, make sure that the steps do not become labored, lack jump, or become earthbound.

# EXERCISE 2

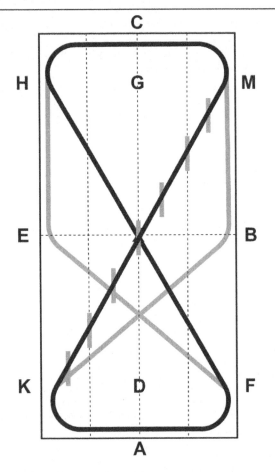

**THE BRIEF:**

Change the rein across the long diagonal (e.g., F-H) or the short diagonal (e.g., F-E)

---

**VARIATIONS:**

- Prevent the horse from anticipating by switching between the long diagonals and short diagonals.
- Ride transitions when crossing the center line (e.g., trot-walk-trot, trot-halt-trot, canter-trot-canter, simple changes, and flying changes)
- Ride extensions across the diagonal (e.g., medium trot, extended canter)
- Ride lateral movements across the diagonal (e.g., leg-yield and half-pass)
- Practice halt and immobility when crossing the center line.
- Ride free walk on a long rein on one diagonal, followed by extended strides on another.

---

**NOTES:**

- The horse must stay straight and travel on one track, (unless riding lateral movements)
- Use half-halts to balance the horse and prevent him for falling onto his forehand.
- Don't allow the horse to cut the corners in anticipation of crossing the diagonal. Ride the corners correctly to help bring the horse's inside hind leg underneath him to keep him straight and balanced.

**EXERCISE 3**

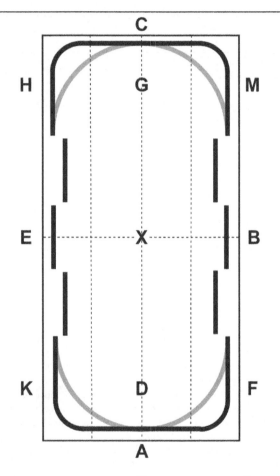

**THE BRIEF:**

Ride down the long side of the arena, push the horse off the track, and then back onto the track, then off the track, and back onto the track.

Note that you do not need to touch the quarter line, you are simply coming onto an inside track.

---

**VARIATIONS:**

- The exercise can be ridden in walk, trot, canter.
- You can push the horse's whole body off the track (leg-yield), you can push just the shoulders off the track (shoulder-in), you can push just the quarters off the track (travers), or you can do a combination of all three.
- To decrease the difficulty, you can push the horse off the track only once rather than twice.

---

**NOTES:**

- The horse must continue to travel down the long side of the arena in the same rhythm and tempo, and with a forward thought.
- When leg-yielding keep a slight flexion away from the direction of travel, and bring the horse on and off the track using your legs, not your reins.
- When riding shoulder-in and travers, maintain the correct positioning through the horse's body and make a clear distinction between travelling straight and travelling laterally.

# EXERCISE 4

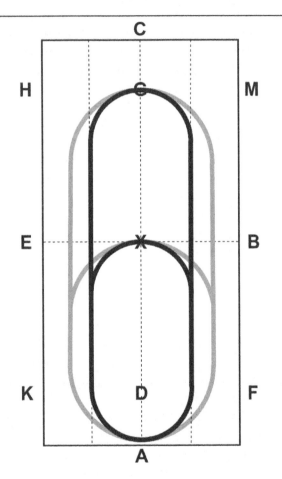

**THE BRIEF:**

Ride along the quarter lines with half 10-meter circles going through X and G.

---

**VARIATIONS:**

- For younger horses or those at the beginning of their training, make the shape bigger. Ride half 15-meter circles, as opposed to 10-meter circles to help the horse keep his balance.
- Ride transitions over G and X (e.g., walk-trot, trot-canter, canter-trot).
- Ride extended strides on the straight lines (e.g., medium trot, extended walk, and ride collected strides on the half circles).
- Ride shoulder-in and/or travers on the straight lines.
- To decrease the difficulty, ride the exercise going down the center line and along the outside track rather than in the center of the arena.

---

**NOTES:**

- Look up and ahead around the circles to ensure that you hit the line you want and don't overshoot it.
- Keep the horse straight and travelling on one track on the quarter lines, unless riding lateral exercises.
- If riding shoulder-in and/or travers, use the half 10-meter circle to help position your horse and ensure the horse keeps moving forward in the same rhythm and tempo.

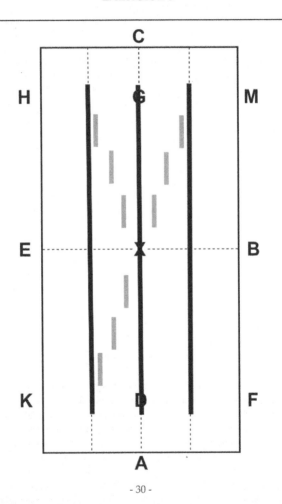

**THE BRIEF:**

Ride straight lines down the center line and the quarter lines.

---

**VARIATIONS:**

- You can ride this exercise in all variations of the paces, (e.g., working trot, collected canter, extended walk, etc). You can ride medium strides down one line and collected strides down another line.
- Incorporate transitions on the straight lines when passing X (e.g., trot-walk-trot, working canter to collected canter and back to working canter, canter -walk-canter).
- For added difficulty, ride shoulder-in and travers down the lines.
- Ride lateral exercises to move from one line to another, e.g., leg-yield from the quarter line to the center line.

---

**NOTES:**

- This exercise tests straightness and accuracy. Keep the horse in front of your leg and moving forward to help maintain the straightness.
- When riding on the quarter lines, ensure that your horse doesn't drift back to the outside track. Use your outside rein and outside leg to keep the horse on the desired line.
- If riding shoulder-in and/or travers, aim for quality rather than quantity. Ride as many correctly positioned and balanced steps as the horse is capable of, then straighten and ride to the end of the arena.

# EXERCISE 6

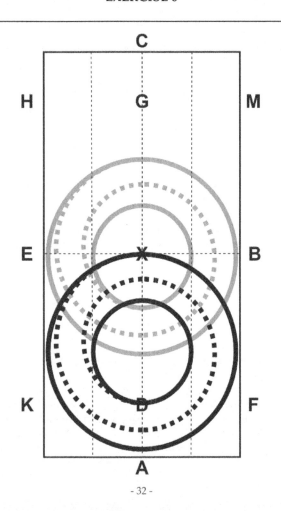

**THE BRIEF:**

Ride a 20-meter circle, spiral in onto a smaller 10-meter circle, and then spiral back out again.

---

**VARIATIONS:**

- Ride the circle in the center of the arena around X for added difficulty.
- Ride medium strides on the larger 20-meter circle and collected strides on the smaller 10-meter circle.
- Ride transitions on the circles, e.g., canter on the large circle and spiral in. Transition to trot when you hit the 10-meter circle. Spiral back out, and ride a transition to canter when you hit the 20-meter circle.
- You can ride the exercise laterally and leg-yield in and out on the circle.

---

**NOTES:**

- Keep a uniform bend through the horse's body, and don't allow him to fall in or fall out.
- Ensure that you remain sitting up straight and in the center of the saddle. Don't collapse at the waist or lean inwards.
- Pay attention to arena geometry to make sure that your circles are of the correct size, are equal, and are round. Use cones to help accuracy.
- Maintain the impulsion and uphill balance, especially on the smaller circles.
- If riding in canter, make sure that the steps do not become labored, lack jump, or become earthbound.

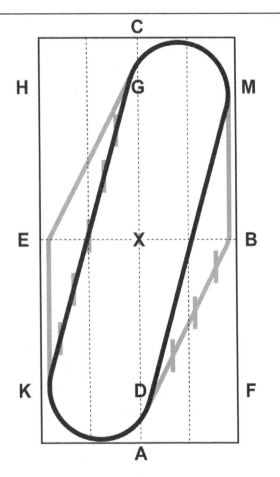

## THE BRIEF:

Ride straight lines from the center line to a corner marker (e.g., A-M and C-K as shown in black) or to a middle marker (e.g., A-B and C-E as shown in grey).

---

## VARIATIONS:

- Ride lengthened strides, medium, and extended paces on the straight lines, collecting and rebalancing the horse through the corners.
- Ride more advanced exercises, such as leg-yield and half-pass, on the straight lines.

---

## NOTES:

- This can be a tricky shape to ride so pay attention to accuracy and make sure you look up and ahead.
- Your horse will stay straighter if he is working nicely forward; horses that are dawdling behind their riders' leg are far more likely to wander on straight lines and drift out on circles and through corners.
- Make sure that your horse is working from both your legs into both reins equally. It can be helpful to envisage that your horse is working along a tunnel created by your leg and rein.
- When riding lengthened strides keep the rhythm and tempo the same, and don't be tempted to fire the horse into the lengthening, as that will cause him to lose his balance, become hollow, and start running.

# EXERCISE 8

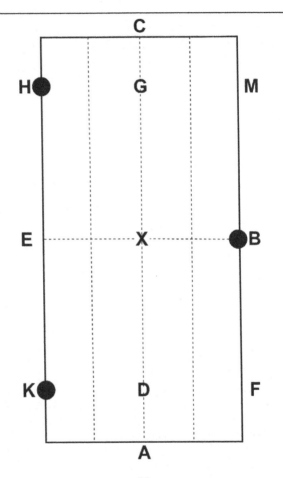

## THE BRIEF:

Choose several spots around the arena.

Each time you ride past one of those spots, ride a transition, change the rein, ride a circle, or ride a lateral movement.

---

## VARIATIONS:

- The more spots you choose, the harder this exercise becomes.
- Transitions can be between the paces, (e.g., walk to trot), or within the paces (e.g., working trot to medium trot).
- Use the letters around the arena, or lay out various cones and buckets to use as markers.
- Use different size circles, depending on your horse's level of training, e.g., 20-meter, 15-meter, 10-meter, and 8-meter circles.
- Ride various lateral movements including leg-yield, shoulder-in, travers, renvers, and half-pass.

---

## NOTES:

- Focus on quality rather than accuracy e.g., if you pass the marker at B, don't halt abruptly. Instead, ride the transition a bit later but ride it well. The aim of this exercise is to keep changing things up, but in order for that to be effective, you must maintain the quality and fluency of your work.
- Pay attention to the transitions and work on having the horse responsive to the legs, seat, and rein aids.

## EXERCISE 9

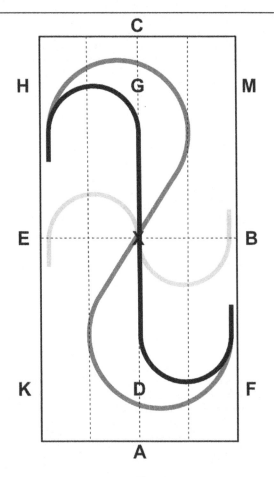

**THE BRIEF:**

Change the rein down the centerline through two half 10-meter circles (shown in black).

Increase the difficulty by riding two half 10-meter circles in the center of the arena (shown in light grey). Decrease the difficulty by riding two half 15-meter circles connected by a straight line over X (shown in dark grey).

---

**VARIATIONS:**

- Ride transitions over X (e.g., trot-walk-trot, trot-halt-trot, canter-trot-canter, simple change, flying change).
- Use the 10-meter circle to position the horse for shoulder-in or travers on the centerline. Remember to straighten the horse before riding the final half 10-meter circle in the opposite direction.
- Ride lengthened, medium, and extended strides on the centerline.
- Ride collected strides on the half circles.

---

**NOTES:**

- If the horse anticipates circling to the left from the centerline, circle to the right, and vice versa.
- Look up and ahead to make sure you don't overshoot the centerline.
- Ensure any transitions that you ride at X are straight and accurate.

## EXERCISE 10

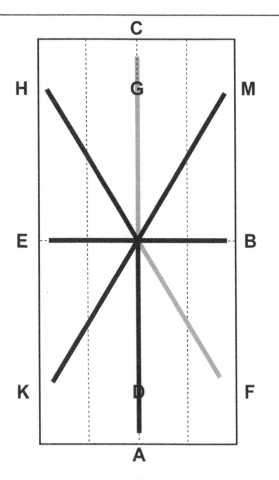

**THE BRIEF:**

Transitions over X on straight lines.

---

**VARIATIONS:**

- Ride through X via a center line or diagonal line.
- You can mix things up and prevent your horse from anticipating the exercise by riding from a diagonal line onto the center line, as shown in grey.
- Transitions you can ride over X include trot-walk-trot, trot-halt-trot, trot-walk, trot-canter, canter-trot-canter, simple changes, and flying changes.

---

**NOTES:**

- Prepare yourself and your horse for the transitions to ensure that they are accurate and happen at X. Use cones for guidance if you need to.
- This exercise is a test of straightness. Keep the horse thinking forward and moving on one track.
- If your horse begins to anticipate a transition at X, ride the transitions either before or after X.
- A good downward transition should feel smooth, not bumpy and rough, and the horse should feel light in your hands as he steps under with his hind legs.
- In a good upwards transition, you should feel your horse's back lifting underneath you as he pushes himself forward with his hind legs, steps underneath his body, and his center of gravity changes.

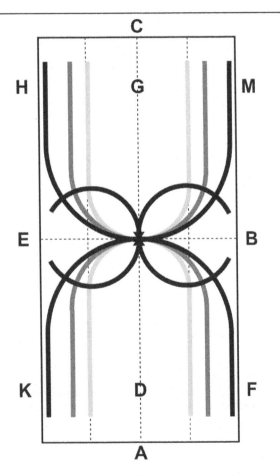

**THE BRIEF:**

Transitions over X on a curved line.

---

**VARIATIONS:**

- Ride through X using one of the curved lines shown on a 20-meter curve, a 15-meter curve, or a 10-meter curve.
- You can make the transition and stay on the same rein, or follow the opposite curve and change the rein.
- Transitions you can ride over X include trot-walk-trot, trot-halt-trot, trot-walk, trot-canter, canter-trot-canter, simple changes, and flying changes.

---

**NOTES:**

- Prepare yourself and your horse for the transitions to ensure that they are accurate and happen at X.
- Prevent the horse from falling in or falling out on the circle by keeping him securely between your inside leg and outside rein.
- Look up and ahead of you to ensure that the circle stays round and doesn't morph into an oval.
- A good downward transition should feel smooth, not bumpy and rough, and the horse should feel light in your hands as he steps under with his hind legs.
- In a good upwards transition, you should feel your horse's back lifting underneath you as he pushes himself forward with his hind legs, steps underneath his body, and his center of gravity changes.

# EXERCISE 12

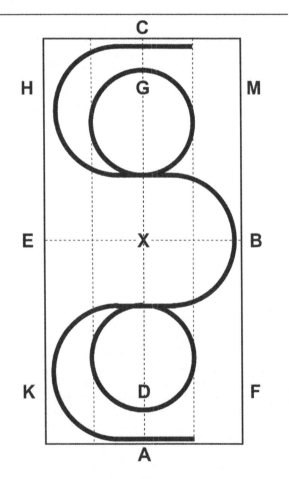

**THE BRIEF:**

Ride a three-loop serpentine with two 10-meter circles.

---

**VARIATIONS:**

- This is an excellent exercise for practicing counter-canter. You will start and finish on the correct lead while riding counter-canter past B (or E if you ride this exercise on the opposite rein).
- Ride working trot through the serpentine and collected trot on the 10-meter circles.
- You can ride transitions at B (or E), e.g., trot-walk-trot, trot-halt-trot.

---

**NOTES:**

- Maintain the accuracy of the 10-meter circles, as they may feel that they are ridden in 'no man's land.' Use cones or buckets to help if you need to.
- To ride an accurate three-loop serpentine, imagine splitting the arena into three equal parts.
- The exercise should be a series of curves and circles with no sharp turns or corners. The whole movement should flow.
- If riding the exercise in canter, ensure that you maintain the impulsion and jump of the pace. Don't allow the canter to become a shuffle.
- To prevent your horse from changing leads in counter-canter, you need to maintain the bend to the leading leg and keep control of the shoulder.

## EXERCISE 13

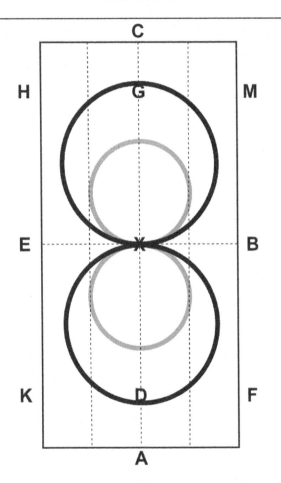

**THE BRIEF:**

A figure of eight at X made up of 15-meter circles and/or 10-meter circles in the center of the arena.

---

**VARIATIONS:**

- Ride two 15-meter circles, two 10-meter circles, or mix it up and ride a 15-meter circle to a 10-meter circle.
- Ride the smaller circles in a collected pace and the larger circles in a working pace. (e.g., 10-meter circle left in collected canter, transition to trot at X, and 15-meter circle to the right in trot.)

---

**NOTES:**

- Maintain the accuracy of the circles. That's more difficult than it sounds because you are riding in the center of the arena, so use cones for guidance if you need to.
- Use your outside rein and outside leg to prevent your horse from drifting back onto the track, especially on the 15-meter circle.
- Keep a uniform bend through the horse's body and maintain the impulsion and uphill balance, especially on the smaller circles.
- Ensure that you remain sitting up straight and in the center of the saddle. Don't collapse at the waist or lean inwards.
- When riding in and out of a collected pace, maintain the same rhythm, tempo, and energy; collection does not mean 'go slower'.

# EXERCISE 14

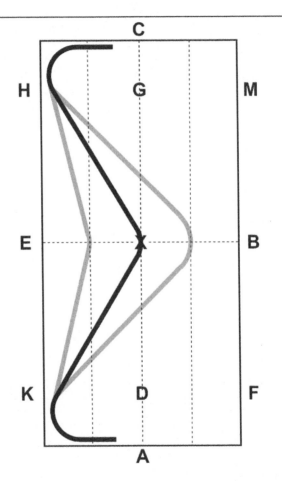

**THE BRIEF:**

Ride a 10-meter loop down the long side of the arena (drawn in black).

The difficulty can be decreased by riding a 5-meter loop or increased by riding a 15-meter loop.

---

**VARIATIONS:**

- The shallow loops can be ridden in canter as a training exercise for counter-canter.
- Ride the first part of the loop in shoulder-in. Change the bend as you hit the deepest part of the curve, and ride the second part of the loop in travers.

---

**NOTES:**

- The exercise should be a series of smooth curves and changes of bend with no sharp turns or corners.
- Ensure that the loops are symmetrical in shape and length.
- Maintain the accuracy, and be sure to hit the quarter line, centerline, or three-quarter line.
- If you're riding the loops in rising trot, it's advised that you change your diagonal as you ask your horse to change the bend. That helps your horse stay balanced and makes your intentions clearer.
- To prevent your horse from changing leads in counter-canter, you need to maintain the bend to the leading leg and keep control of the shoulder.

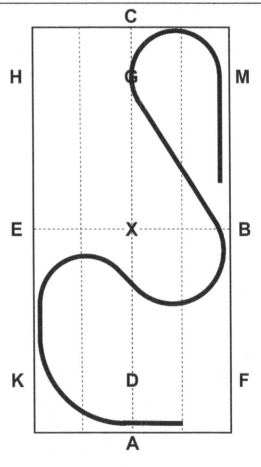

**THE BRIEF:**

Ride a half 10-meter circle at M and re-join the track at B. Then, ride a flowing S-bend to re-join the track before K.

This is a very strange shape, and although it can be ridden in all three paces, it's ideally suited to training counter-canter.

---

**VARIATIONS:**

*   If your horse is new to counter-canter, ride the S-bend flatter.
*   If your horse is established in counter-canter, then ride the S-bend deeper to increase the difficulty of the exercise.

---

**NOTES:**

*   If riding the exercise in rising trot, remember to change your diagonal every time you ask the horse to change the bend.
*   To prevent your horse from changing leads in counter-canter, you need to maintain the bend to the leading leg and keep control of the shoulder.
*   You should not get carried away and ride too much counter canter all at once. It is a good idea to intersperse the counter canter with some trot and true canter to revisit the impulsion and to enable you to feel the thoroughness and carriage building.
*   Maintain the same rhythm and tempo throughout the exercise.

# EXERCISE 16

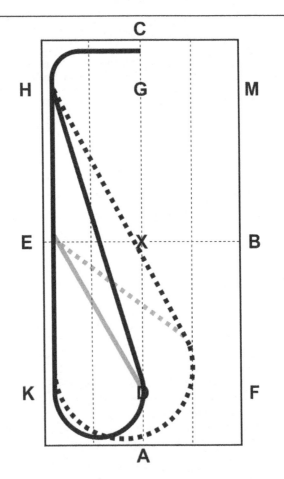

**THE BRIEF:**

Ride a half 10-meter circle at K, returning to the track at either H or E.

---

**VARIATIONS:**

- On the long side of the arena or on the line back to the track, ride lengthened, medium, or extended strides.
- On the line back to the track, ride leg-yield or half-pass.
- On the long side of the arena, ride shoulder-in or travers.
- Decrease the difficulty by riding a half 15-meter circle instead of a half 10-meter circle, as shown by the dotted lines.

---

**NOTES:**

- Look up and ahead to make sure that your half circle is accurate and you hit the desired line.
- Before re-joining the outside track, remember to ride a half-halt to rebalance the horse, change the bend, and change your diagonal if in rising trot.
- If leg-yielding back to the track, ride a few straight strides after the half-circle before commencing the leg yield.
- If riding half-pass back to the track, use the half-circle to help position the horse correctly.
- When riding lengthened strides keep the rhythm and tempo the same, and don't be tempted to fire the horse into the lengthening, as that will cause him to lose his balance, become hollow, and start running.

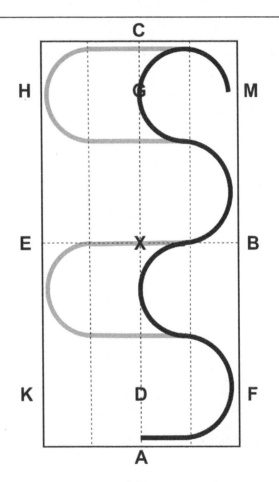

**THE BRIEF:**

Ride a serpentine made up of half 10-meter circles down one half of the arena, as shown in black.

In a short 20mx40m arena, that gives you a 4-loop serpentine, as pictured. In a long 20m x 60m arena, you would ride a 6-loop serpentine.

---

**VARIATIONS:**

- To decrease the difficulty, you can ride a full 4-loop serpentine to each side of the arena, as shown in grey. That gives you more time to change the bend and helps to keep your horse balanced.
- Ride a transition every half circle. E.g., ride the first half circle in walk, the second half-circle in trot, the third half-circle in walk, and the fourth half-circle in trot.

---

**NOTES:**

- If in rising trot, remember to change your diagonal when changing the bend.
- Make sure the horse has a uniform bend to each direction, and all half-circles are of equal size.
- Ensure the horse is bending throughout his whole body, not just in the neck.
- Guard the quarters with your outside leg to prevent them from swinging out on the half-circles.

# EXERCISE 18

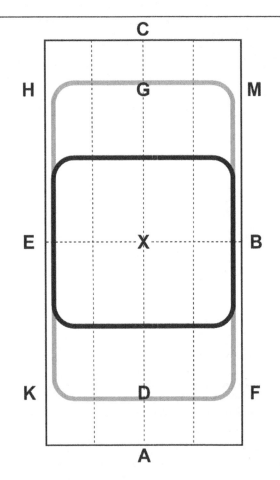

**THE BRIEF:**

Ride a square made up of straight lines and deep, almost right-angled corners in the center of the arena.

---

**VARIATIONS:**

- Instead of riding a square, you can ride a rectangle by going further down the long sides of the arena, as shown in grey.
- Ride a quarter walk pirouette at each corner.
- Ride a quarter canter pirouette at each corner.
- Ride a square halt when crossing the center line. Immobility for 5 seconds. Proceed in walk or trot.
- Ride transitions before and after the corners. E.g., ride working trot on a straight line, just before the corner, transition to medium walk. Ride the corner, then transition back into working trot.

---

**NOTES:**

- If riding a walk pirouette, make sure that the 4-beat sequence of the walk is maintained, and the tempo of the walk remains the same throughout.
- If riding a canter pirouette, maintain the quality and the impulsion of the canter with the horse clearly taking the weight onto the hind legs.
- When riding straight lines, remember to ride forward to help keep the horse straight and moving on one track. Consciously feel that you have equal weight in both seat bones and equal weight in both reins.

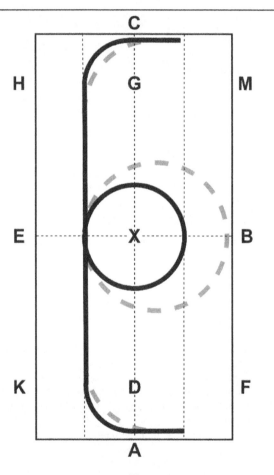

## THE BRIEF:

Ride down a quarter line, and ride a 10-meter circle around X, touching the opposite quarter line.

---

## VARIATIONS:

- Ride the quarter line in a working pace and the circle in a collected pace (e.g., working trot down the quarter line, 10-meter circle in collected trot, then working trot to the end of the arena).
- Ride shoulder-in and/or travers on the quarter line (e.g., in working trot, turn left onto the quarter line at C and ride shoulder-in left. Ride a 10-meter circle left, then ride travers left to the end of the arena).
- To decrease the difficulty, ride a shallower corner onto the quarter line and ride a 15-meter circle instead of a 10-meter circle.

---

## NOTES:

- Straightness on the quarter line is key to riding an accurate 10-meter circle in the center.
- When riding the 10-meter circle, it's your job to choose the right tempo (speed of the rhythm) so that the horse makes the small circle without any disturbances to the rhythm or unevenness in stride length.
- If riding shoulder-in and/or travers, use the preceding corners and the 10-meter circle to position the horse correctly.

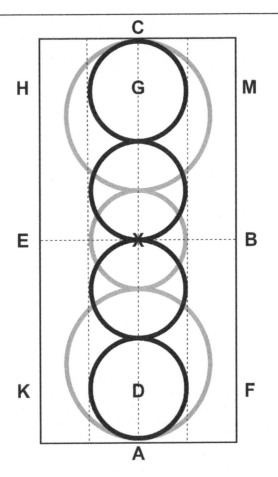

## THE BRIEF:

Ride a series of 10-meter circles down the center of the arena. You will have to ride 1.5 revolutions of each circle before changing the rein and moving onto the next circle.

If you are in a short 20mx40m arena, you will ride four 10-meter circles, as pictured. If you are in a long 20mx60m arena, you will ride six 10-meter circles.

---

## VARIATIONS:

- Ride each circle in a different pace. E.g., ride the first circle in walk, the second circle in trot, the third circle in walk, and the fourth circle in canter.
- To decrease the difficulty, replace the 10-meter circles with 15-meter circles where possible. In a long 20mx60m arena, ride three 15-meter circles, but in a short 20mx40m arena, ride two 15-meter circles with a 10-meter circle, as pictured in grey.

---

## NOTES:

- When riding the 10-meter circles, it's your job to choose the right tempo (speed of the rhythm) so that the horse can manage the circles without any disturbances in rhythm or unevenness in stride length.
- If riding in canter, make sure that the steps do not become labored, lack jump, or become earthbound.

# EXERCISE 21

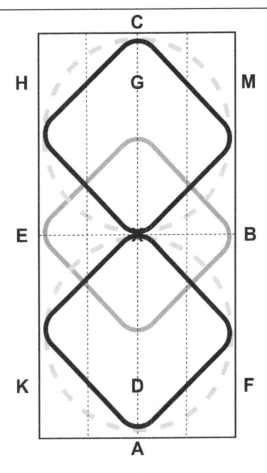

**THE BRIEF:**

Rather than riding a 20-meter circle, picture a square in the middle and ride straight from corner to corner.

This is a good exercise for horses that tend to fall in or fall out on circles or if you need help with riding an accurately shaped circle.

---

**VARIATIONS:**

- To increase the difficulty, ride the square in the center of the arena around X, as pictured in grey.
- Ride transitions on the straight lines (e.g., trot-walk-trot).
- Ride transitions in the corners (e.g., ride in working trot and transition to canter in one of the corners).

---

**NOTES:**

- Use a half-halt to prepare and balance the horse before each corner.
- Guard your horse's shoulders and quarters with your outside aids to prevent the horse from drifting out on the corners.
- Visualize where all the four 'corners' are before you begin the exercise to make sure you ride an accurate shape. You can use cones and buckets to guide you.
- Make it clear that you are riding straight, then riding a corner, and then riding straight again, rather than drifting around the shape.

# EXERCISE 22

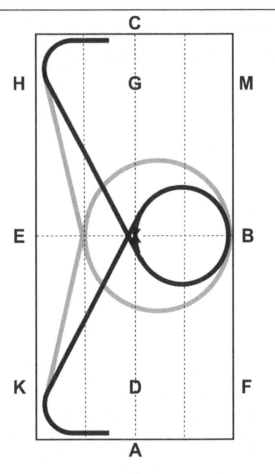

**THE BRIEF:**

Ride from a corner marker to X. Once you reach X, ride a 10-meter circle on the same rein before riding to the corner marker at the other end of the arena.

---

**VARIATIONS:**

- Ride medium strides to X, and ride collected strides on the circle (e.g., medium canter K-X, then 10-meter circle right in collected canter, then medium canter to H).
- Leg-yield to X before riding the 10-meter circle, then leg-yield back to the track.
- To decrease the difficulty, ride to the quarter line and ride a 15-meter circle rather than a 10-meter circle, as pictured in grey.

---

**NOTES:**

- Ride a half-halt before X to balance the horse and move his weight back onto his hindquarters, ready for the 10-meter circle.
- If leg-yielding, aim to hit the centerline a stride before X. That will give you enough time to change the bend before the 10-meter circle.
- Ensure that you remain sitting up straight and in the center of the saddle. Don't collapse at the waist or lean inwards on the circle.
- Ensure the horse has a uniform bend through his whole body on the circle and in the corners.

# EXERCISE 23

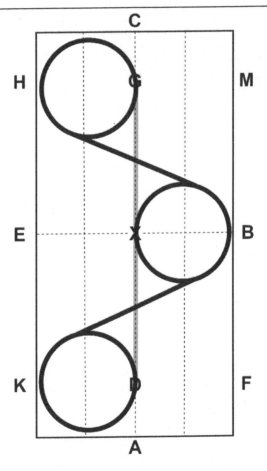

**THE BRIEF:**

Ride three 10-meter circles at alternating sides of the arena, connecting each of them by a diagonal line.

---

**VARIATIONS:**

- You can connect the circles via the centerline rather than a diagonal line, as shown in grey.
- Ride a transition between each circle (e.g., ride the circle near K in working trot. When approaching the circle near B, ride a trot-walk-trot transition).
- Ride the circles in canter, and change the canter lead between the circles by riding canter-trot-canter, a simple change, or a flying change.

---

**NOTES:**

- Use half-halts to keep the horse balanced throughout the exercise, especially before and after transitions and when changing the horse's bend.
- When riding the 10-meter circles, it's your job to choose the right tempo (speed of the rhythm) so that the horse can perform the circles without any disturbances to the rhythm or unevenness in stride length.
- When bending correctly, the horse should remain on one track and he should bend uniformly through his body and neck in the direction of travel, and should not tip or tilt his head against the correct flexion.

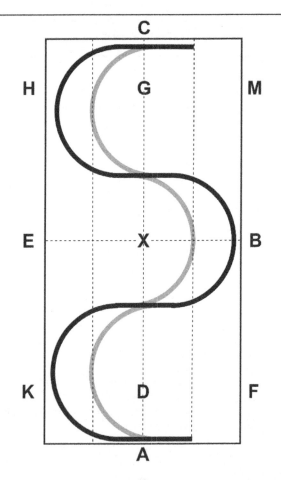

**THE BRIEF:**

Ride a three-loop serpentine.

---

**VARIATIONS:**

- To increase the difficulty, ride the serpentine down the center of the arena, touching the quarter lines rather than the outside track, as pictured in grey.
- Ride a transition each time you cross the center line (e.g., trot-walk, trot-walk-trot, trot-halt-trot, trot-canter, canter-trot, canter-trot-canter, simple change, flying change).
- Ride a transition to halt as you cross the centerline or at B. Immobility for 5 seconds, then proceed in walk or trot.

---

**NOTES:**

- The exercise should be a series of smooth curves and bends, with no sharp turns.
- Ensure the three loops are of equal size and shape. Imagine splitting the arena up into three equal parts.
- When asking your horse to bend around the curves, use your inside leg on the girth to encourage the horse to bend around it, and keep your outside leg on as a passive aid to prevent the quarters from swinging out.
- The rhythm of the pace should remain consistent throughout the exercise, and the horse should not speed up or slow down as he negotiates each loop.

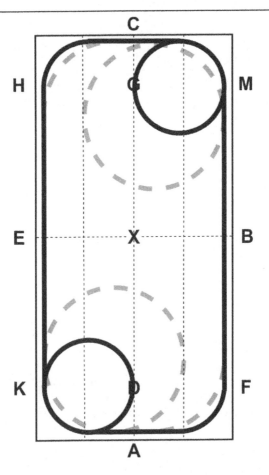

**THE BRIEF:**

Go around the outside of the arena and ride a 10-meter circle in the corner *before* going down the long side.

So, if riding on the right rein, you will ride a circle in the C-M corner and the A-K corner. If riding on the left rein, you will ride a circle in the C-H corner and the A-F corner.

---

**VARIATIONS:**

- Ride the 10-meter circles in a collected pace before riding lengthened, medium, or extended strides down the long side of the arena.
- Ride transitions on the long sides (e.g., trot-walk-trot, trot-halt followed by rein-back before proceeding in trot).
- Ride shoulder-in or travers down the long side of the arena (e.g., 10-meter circle right in the C-M corner, then travers right from M-B. Followed by another 10-meter circle in the A-K corner, then shoulder-in right from K-H).
- To decrease the difficulty, ride 15-meter circles instead of 10-meter circles as pictured in grey.

---

**NOTES:**

- When riding the circles, remember to have even bend through the horse's body, from the tail, centrally through the hindquarters, through the back and shoulders, through the neck, finishing at the poll. There should be no head tilting.

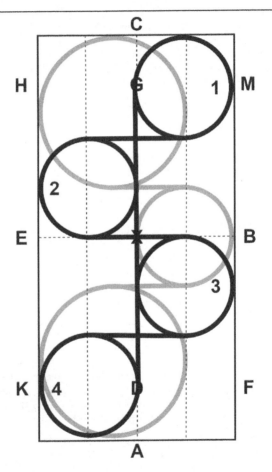

**THE BRIEF:**

Ride a series of 10-meter circles on alternating sides of the arena connected by a serpentine or by the centerline.

If you are in a short 20mx40m arena, you will ride four 10-meter circles, as pictured in black. If you are in a long 20mx60m arena, you will ride six 10-meter circles.

---

**VARIATIONS:**

- You can mix and match the circles and ride them in any order to prevent your horse from anticipating (e.g., ride circle 1, then go down the centerline and ride circle 4, then across to circle 3, then across to circle 2, and finally, back down the centerline to circle 4).
- To decrease the difficulty, ride 15-meter circles where possible. In a long 20mx60m arena, you can ride four 15-meter circles. In a short 20mx40m arena, you can ride two 15-meter circles and one 10-meter circle or loop, as pictured in grey.

---

**NOTES:**

- If riding in riding trot, remember to change your diagonal each time you change the bend and direction of travel.
- Ensure the horse bends uniformly and equally on both reins.
- Sit up and don't lean to the inside. Look ahead to help you maintain accuracy.

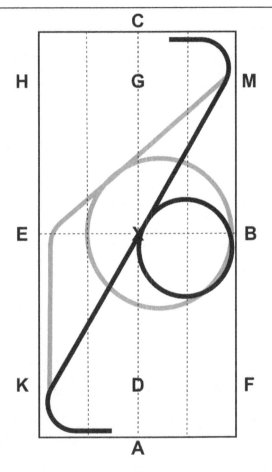

**THE BRIEF:**

Ride across the long diagonal. Once you reach X, ride a 10-meter circle before continuing along the diagonal.

---

**VARIATIONS:**

- Ride the exercise in canter, changing the lead via a canter-trot-canter transition, a simple change, or a flying change when you reach the other side of the arena, (or before X, depending on which way you decide to tackle this exercise).
- Ride in a working pace, transitioning to a collected pace for the 10-meter circle.
- Ride leg-yield or half-pass along the diagonal line (e.g., leg-yield from K-X, 10-meter circle right, half-pass from X-M).
- You can decrease the difficulty by going across the short diagonal and riding a 15-meter circle instead of a 10-meter circle as pictured in grey.

---

**NOTES:**

- Pay attention to the accuracy of the 10-meter circle at X. Notice that it is not centered at either X or B.
- Use the circle in the middle of the arena to help you re-engage the horse's hindquarters.
- Use half-halts to balance the horse both before and after the circle.
- Maintain the same rhythm and tempo throughout the exercise; the horse should not slow down to negotiate the circle.

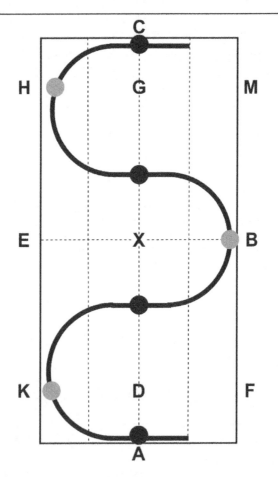

## THE BRIEF:

Ride a 3-loop serpentine with a transition each time you cross the center line, as marked by the black dots.

---

## VARIATIONS:

- You can ride indirect transitions (e.g., walk-trot), direct transitions (e.g., walk-canter, trot-halt), or transitions between the paces (e.g., working trot-collected trot-working trot).
- You can decrease the difficulty of the exercise by riding the transitions when on the outside track, as marked by the grey dots, instead of down the center line. Riding the transition next to the arena boundary with a clear bend will help to balance the horse.

---

## NOTES:

- When riding the transitions across the centerline, ensure that the horse remains on one track and the quarters do not drift left or right.
- Upward transitions should be obedient and responsive but remain fluid and smooth.
- Downward transitions should remain forward and in self-carriage, without the horse stopping abruptly or tipping onto the forehand.
- Prepare for the transitions using a half-halt and aim for an accurate transition as your upper body crosses the center line.

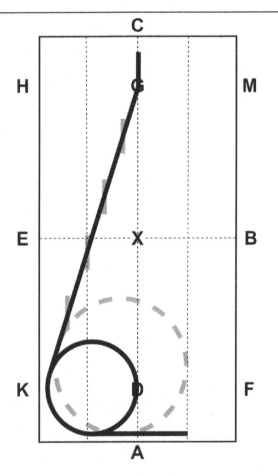

**THE BRIEF:**

Turn down the centerline and then ride toward one of the corner markers at the opposite end of the school before commencing a 10-meter circle in the corner.

---

**VARIATIONS:**

- Ride leg-yield or half-pass along the diagonal line.
- Ride lengthened, medium, or extended paces down the diagonal line before collecting the pace ready for the circle.
- To decrease the difficulty of the exercise, you can ride a 15-meter circle instead of a 10-meter circle.

---

**NOTES:**

- Guard the shoulders and quarters on the circle so that the horse doesn't evade the bend by drifting out.
- Keep a uniform bend through the horse's body and maintain the impulsion and uphill balance.
- Ensure that you remain sitting up straight and in the center of the saddle. Don't collapse at the waist or lean inwards.
- The rhythm must be correct and in a suitable tempo (speed) and must stay consistent throughout the exercise.
- When riding lengthened strides don't be tempted to fire the horse into the lengthening, as that will cause him to lose his balance, become hollow, and start running.
- When riding in and out of a collected pace, maintain the same rhythm, tempo, and energy; collection does not mean 'go slower'.

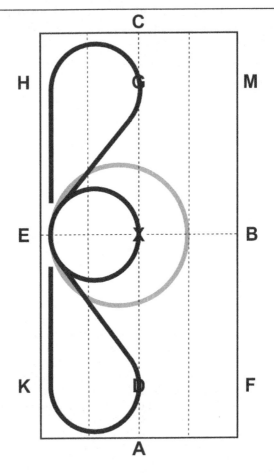

**THE BRIEF:**

Ride down the long side of the arena and ride a half 10-meter circle in the corner and re-join the track again at either B or E on the opposite rein.

Ride a 10-meter circle before heading towards either D or G and riding another half 10-meter circle in the corner to re-join the outside track on the same rein as which you started.

---

**VARIATIONS:**

- Decrease the difficulty of the exercise by riding a 15-meter circle instead of a 10-meter circle, as pictured in grey.
- Ride a few lengthened or medium strides on the long side and/or diagonal line to freshen up the pace.
- Ride shoulder-in on the long side, picking up travers as you ride the diagonal, straightening the horse before you begin the circle.

---

**NOTES:**

- Look up and ahead around the circle and half-circle to ensure that you hit the line you want and don't overshoot it.
- Keep the horse straight and travelling on one track on, unless riding lateral exercises.
- Use half-halts to help balance the horse for each change of bend and change of direction. If riding in rising trot, remember to change your diagonal too.

# GLOSSARY

This section gives you a brief overview of dressage terminology and movements.

For more detailed information of how to train and ride these movements, along with uncovering what the dressage judges are looking for, visit our website HowToDressage.com

---

## PACES

---

**Walk** – The walk has a four-beat rhythm, during which the horse's legs move in the following sequence: left hind, left fore, right hind, right fore. There is no moment of suspension.

**Trot** - The trot has a two-beat rhythm, during which the horse's alternate diagonal legs move in the following sequence: left fore and right hind together, right fore and left hind together. There should be a clear moment of suspension when all the horse's feet are off the floor.

**Canter** – The canter has a three-beat rhythm. True canter means that the horse appears to lead with the inside foreleg. In right canter, the sequence is: left hind, diagonal pair of right hind and left fore, right fore. A clear moment of suspension follows that sequence. In left canter, the sequence is reversed.

**Passage** – Passage is an elevated trot. The horse's legs are raised and returned to the ground in diagonal pairs with a clear moment of prolonged suspension. The toe of the raised forefoot should be level with the center of the cannon bone on the supporting leg. The toe of the raised hind foot should be slightly above the fetlock of the other supporting leg.

**Piaffe** – Piaffe is an advanced dressage movement, which is, essentially, an highly collected and cadenced trot on the spot. The legs move in diagonal pairs with a moment of suspension between. At Intermediare level, one meter of forward travel is permitted per ten steps of piaffe.

---

# VARIATIONS OF PACE

---

**Medium walk** - Medium walk has a four-beat rhythm, during which the horse's legs move in the following sequence: left hind, left fore, right hind, right fore. There is no moment of suspension. The horse should march forward with purposeful, active steps.

**Free walk on a long rein** – Free walk has a four-beat rhythm, during which the horse's legs move in the following sequence: left hind, left fore, right hind, right fore. There is no moment of suspension. The horse should be relaxed and have complete freedom to lower and stretch his head and neck as he follows the rider's hand. The hind feet should clearly overtrack the prints left by the forefeet, and the horse should march forward with purpose.

**Extended walk** – Extended walk has a four-beat rhythm, during which the horse's legs move in the following sequence: left hind, left fore, right hind, right fore. There is no moment of suspension. The horse marches forward with purpose, reaching forward and extending his neck as he seeks the bit but without his poll dropping. The strides cover maximum ground, and the hind feet should overtrack the prints left by the forefeet.

**Collected Walk** – Collected walk has a four-beat rhythm, during which the horse's legs move in the following sequence: left hind, left fore, right hind, right fore. There is no moment of suspension. The steps are shorter, more elevated, and more active than in medium walk. The horse's hind feet should imprint slightly behind or in the prints made by the forefeet.

**Working trot** – Working trot has a two-beat rhythm, during which the horse's alternate diagonal legs move in the following sequence: left fore and right hind together, right fore and left hind together. There should be a clear moment of suspension when all the horse's feet are off the floor. A good quality working trot sees the horse working with active hind legs, propelling himself freely forward through a swinging back. The horse should clearly track-up, which means that the horse's hind feet should step into the prints left by his front feet.

**Collected trot** - Collected trot has a two-beat rhythm, during which the horse's alternate diagonal legs move in the following sequence: left fore and right hind together, right fore and left hind together. There should be a clear moment of suspension when all the horse's feet are off the floor. The horse's steps are energetic, shortened, and elevated, and he takes more weight onto his hindquarters to lift his forehand.

**Medium trot** - Medium trot has a two-beat rhythm, during which the horse's alternate diagonal legs move in the following sequence: left fore and right hind together, right fore and left hind together. There should be a clear moment of suspension when all the horse's feet are off the floor. The horse lengthens his stride equally in front and behind to cover more ground, also lengthening his frame as he does so, with his nose slightly in front of the vertical.

**Extended trot -** Extended trot has a two-beat rhythm, during which the horse's alternate diagonal legs move in the following sequence: left fore and right hind together, right fore and left hind together. There should be a clear moment of suspension when all the horse's feet are off the floor. The horse lengthens his stride to its maximum, covering as much ground as possible. The frame is lengthened so that the horse's nose is in front of the vertical. The hind legs and forelegs should lengthen equally.

**Working canter -** The working canter has a three-beat rhythm. True working canter means that the horse appears to lead with the inside foreleg. In right working canter, the sequence is: left hind, diagonal pair of right hind and left fore, right fore. A clear moment of suspension follows that sequence. In left working canter, the sequence is reversed. There is a steady and even rhythm with a plenty of impulsion and 'jump' to the strides.

**Collected canter –** The collected canter has a three-beat rhythm. True collected canter means that the horse appears to lead with the inside foreleg. In right collected canter, the sequence is: left hind, diagonal pair of right hind and left fore, right fore. A clear moment of suspension follows that sequence. In left collected canter, the sequence is reversed. The stride length is shorter, and the steps have more elevation than in the working canter. The horse's weight is more on the hindquarters, and the outline is higher.

**Medium canter -** The medium canter has a three-beat rhythm. True medium canter means that the horse appears to lead with the inside foreleg. In right medium canter, the sequence is: left hind, diagonal pair of right hind and left fore, right fore. A clear moment of suspension follows that sequence. In left medium canter, the sequence is reversed. The horse lengthens his stride to cover more ground, lengthening his frame as he does so, with his nose slightly in front of the vertical.

**Extended canter** – The extended canter has a three-beat rhythm. True extended canter means that the horse appears to lead with the inside foreleg. In right extended canter, the sequence is: left hind, diagonal pair of right hind and left fore, right fore. A clear moment of suspension follows that sequence. In left medium canter, the sequence is reversed. The horse lengthens his stride to its maximum, covering as much ground as possible. The frame is lengthened so that the horse's nose is in front of the vertical.

# LATERAL MOVEMENTS

**Shoulder-fore** – The horse's forehand is brought slightly in at a shallow angle so that the inside foreleg travels to the inside. The inside hind leg tracks between the imprints of both forelegs. The horse is flexed very slightly to the inside. Shoulder-fore can be ridden in walk, trot, and canter.

**Shoulder-in** – The horse's forehand comes in at an angle of about 30 degrees. The horse is bent away from the direction of travel with a uniform bend through his body. The outside foreleg and inside hind leg follow the same track, while the inside fore and outside hind travel along their own tracks. Shoulder-in can be ridden in walk, trot, and canter.

**Leg-yield** – The horse moves forward and sideways on two tracks with slight flexion of the head and neck away from the direction of travel and his body parallel to the track. The inside feet step across and in front of the outside feet.

**Travers** – The horse is bent in the direction of travel with a uniform bend through his body. The outside legs pass and cross in front of the inside legs so that the horse travels on four tracks at an angle of around 35 degrees. Travers can be ridden in walk, trot, and canter.

**Renvers** – The horse's shoulders are brought to the inside track while the hindquarters remain on the outside track. The horse's body is uniformly bent around the rider's outside leg toward the direction of travel. The horse's front legs remain on their own individual tracks to the inside of the two tracks made by the hind legs. The angle should be around 35 degrees, and the horse should move in four tracks. Renvers can be ridden in walk, trot, and canter.

**Half-pass** – The horse is uniformly bent in the direction of travel. His body should move almost parallel to the track, and the shoulders should be around one hoofprint in front of the haunches. In a trot half-pass, the horse's legs cross over. In a canter half-pass, it should appear as if the horse jumps into the air before landing and repeating.

---

# CHANGES OF CANTER LEAD

---

**Change of lead through trot** – A series of transitions; canter-trot-canter, through which the horse changes canter leads.

**Simple change** – A series of transitions; canter-walk-canter, through which the horse changes canter leads.

**Flying change** – The horse changes canter leads without making any transitions. In a flying change from left to right, the left hind provides support and balance, the right hind jumps through during the moment of suspension, and the right fore and hind legs are at the same height during the moment of the change. The horse remains straight so that the right hind jumps through into the prints of the right fore.

## SCHOOL MOVEMENTS

**Loops** – Loops are ridden between the corner markers and coming in from the track, typically to a depth of 3 meters, 5 meters, and 10 meters, from the long side. Loops can be ridden in walk, trot, and canter.

**Serpentine** – A serpentine is a movement of typically three or four loops, each loop going to the side of the arena and ridden from A or C. The exercise is usually ridden in trot or canter with simple changes or flying changes over the center line.

**Rein-back** – Rein-back is a rearward movement in diagonal pairs. Each pair of legs is raised and returned to the ground alternately, the horse remaining straight and moving on one track. The rhythm is two-beat, and there is no moment of suspension.

**Give and re-take of the reins** – The give and re-take of reins requires the rider to clearly release the contact for one or two strides by moving their hands smoothly forward toward the horse's mouth and then re-taking the contact again.

**Halt** – The horse should stand straight and square with each leg bearing the same weight evenly so that the horse is balanced.

**Circles** – Circles can be any size from 8 meters to 20 meters and may be ridden anywhere in the arena. Circles should be well-shaped and accurate, and the horse should be uniformly bent around the rider's inside leg, moving around the circle on one track.

**Centerline** – The centerline is 10 meters equidistant from each side of the track and runs from A to C.

**Allow the horse to stretch** – This exercise is ridden in rising trot and working canter. The rider allows the horse complete freedom of his back and neck so that he stretches forward through his topline to follow the rider's hand.

**Counter canter** – Counter canter is the opposite of true canter. The horse travels in a three-beat canter sequence, but on the outside lead, e.g., the horse is working on the right rein traveling to the right, but the canter leads with the left fore.

**Canter pirouette** – A canter pirouette is a circle or half-circle on two tracks with a radius that's equal to the horse's length. The forehand moves around the haunches with the forefeet and the outside hind moving around the inside hind to create a pivot. Each time the inside hind leaves the ground, it should return to the same spot. The horse is slightly bent in the direction of the turn.

**Walk pirouette** – A walk pirouette is a turn on the haunches, typically through 180 degrees. The hind legs describe a small circle, ideally around dinner plate size. The hind feet take active, elevated steps, and the clear four-beat walk sequence is maintained. The horse is bent slightly around the rider's inside leg, uniformly throughout his neck and body.

---

# TRANSITIONS

---

**Upward transition** – An upward transition is when the horse transitions from a slower pace to a quicker one, e.g., walk-trot, trot-canter.

**Downward transition** – A downward transition is when the horse transitions from a faster pace to a slower one, e.g., trot-walk, canter-trot, medium trot-collected trot.

**Simple transitions** – A simple transition refer to upward and downward transitions from one pace to another consecutively, e.g., trot-canter, walk-trot, halt-walk.

**Direct transitions** – A direct transition is when the horse transitions from one pace to another, missing out the pace between, e.g., walk-canter, trot-halt.

**Transitions within the paces** – Transitions within the paces refers to transitions made within the same pace, e.g., medium trot-collected trot, working canter-medium canter, free walk-medium walk.

# OTHER RESOURCES

To continue with your dressage training and education, check out our other books and resources.

**How To Dressage (Book 1)**
Our flagship book, How To Dressage (Book 1) outlines the principles of dressage, illustrates correct training, and breaks down dressage movements. Available on Amazon in paperback and e-book format.

**How to Win at Dressage**
This mini e-book looks at simple ways in which any rider can increase their dressage test scores. Available on Amazon in e-book format only.

**The BIG Book of Dressage Exercises**
Over 40 floorplans and 190 dressage exercises (including pole exercises), this 700-page workbook is our #1 bestselling book. Available on Amazon in paperback format only.

**Our Website**
Dressage training is never-ending – and so is our website! New articles are being published every week on HowToDressage.com. To help make sure that you don't miss any, remember to subscribe to our mailing list and follow our Facebook Page.

**Our Training Forum**
We've recently launched a new dressage training forum on our website, and we'd love for you to pop by. As with all forums, there's a place for discussing everything that is dressage,

competitions and horse care. But we also welcome equestrian bloggers and business and encourage them to share their websites, blog posts, products, sales and discounts.

You can join free at HowToDressage.com/Community

**Our Podcast**

Every Monday we release a new episode of the How To Dressage podcast where we break down the How To's of dressage. You can download it for free from Apple Podcasts, Spotify, Google Podcasts and all other major podcast players.

**The Ultimate Training Diaries**

We have a range of dressage and equestrian training diaries to help you take care of your horse, achieve your training goals, and be successful in the competition arena. Available on Amazon in paperback format only.

**Other Free Stuff**

For other training resources, such as free email courses and downloads, visit HowToDressage.com/free-stuff

# Free Email Training Courses

- **Dressage Newbie Email Course** – A course designed for those who are new to dressage.
  https://howtodressage.com/newbiecourse

- **Dressage Competition Email Course** – A course for riders who are new to competitive dressage.
  https://howtodressage.com/competitioncourse

- **Scales of Training Email Course** – A course looking at each of the training scales in depth.
  https://howtodressage.com/scalescourse

# Free Download

- **7 Simples Steps to Boost Your Dressage Scores** –
  https://howtodressage.com/7steps

Made in United States
Orlando, FL
22 November 2022

24835693R00061